A Discourse on Method

53SP 32
August 2020
Brooklyn, NY

53rdstatepress.org

A Discourse on Method is made possible by the New York State Council on the Arts with the support of Governor Andrew M. Cuomo and the New York State Legislature.

Book design: Karinne Keithley Syers

ISBN: 978-0-9978664-5-2
Library of Congress Control Number: 2019948717

Printed in the United States of America

A Discourse on Method

Shonni Enelow and David Levine

53rd State Press
Brooklyn, New York

CONTENTS

His Methods Became Unsound

Shonni Enelow

I BOUGHT A plane ticket to Madison, Wisconsin, in a fit of panic during the summer of 2014. I had actually been in a semi-constant state of panic from the moment I signed my book contract the previous spring, certain that this apparently happy event would result in one way or another in some sort of ornate, shattering downfall, which I imagined in ever more tawdry and megalomaniacal images. But this was different. I hadn't visited the Wisconsin Theater Collection, where the 406 cassette tapes recorded at the Actors Studio between 1956 and 1969 have been housed since Lee Strasberg's death in 1982. I had to go, I told Michael, in the neutral voice of inarguable domestic imperative. I booked a flight from New York to Chicago, where I would change planes for Madison, and arrive at a hotel near the university around 8 pm. I would wake up the next morning and go promptly to the archives, where I would sit in meditative stillness and take rigorous notes for the duration of the work day. I would discover extraordinary things that would raise my argument to new heights by thoroughly corroborating what I already knew. And I would commune with the voice of Lee Strasberg, which would ensconce me in cooling mists of authorial legitimacy.

As we landed in Chicago it began to storm. The plane to Madison was delayed, then delayed again. I waited in the terminal and sent Michael pictures of the sky from my phone. My flight was canceled, and there wasn't another available until the next afternoon, meaning I was going to lose more than half of my time at the archives. I called the only person I knew in Chicago, asked if I could stay the night at his place, and got in a cab.

I met Josh our first year as theater majors at the Tisch School of the Arts at NYU. Two weeks after we started college, we watched the Twin Towers burn from our dorm windows. He made up a bed for me in his living room, pushing aside beer bottles and paperbacks. After he went to sleep, I opened one of the books on the coffee table called *The Gals and Guys of Beverly Hills, 90210*, which described the life practices and moral value systems of Jason Priestley, Shannen Doherty, and Luke Perry.

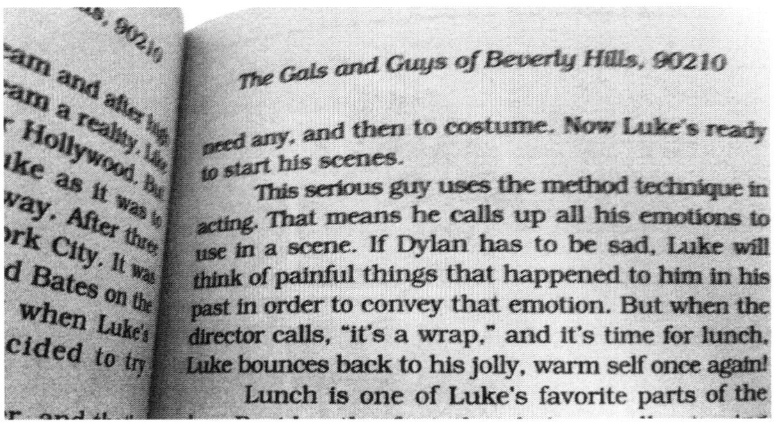

The Gals and Guys of Beverly Hills, 90210

need any, and then to costume. Now Luke's ready to start his scenes.

This serious guy uses the method technique in acting. That means he calls up all his emotions to use in a scene. If Dylan has to be sad, Luke will think of painful things that happened to him in his past in order to convey that emotion. But when the director calls, "it's a wrap," and it's time for lunch, Luke bounces back to his jolly, warm self once again!

Lunch is one of Luke's favorite parts of the

Everything called method acting descends from Constantin Stanislavsky, the Russian impresario of the Moscow Art Theatre, which toured the United States in the 1920s. Its success inspired two members of the company, Richard Boleslavsky and Maria Ouspenskaya, to start the American Laboratory Theatre in New York to teach Stanislavsky's techniques. Among their students were Harold Clurman and Lee Strasberg, who, in 1931, started the Group Theatre to put what they learned into practice. Strasberg, who was in charge of training the actors, developed his own acting technique based on those of Stanislavsky, Boleslavsky, and Ouspenskaya. The Group earned a reputation for idealistic leftist politics and quality ensemble acting, and they're still the template for the utopian theater collectives that invade American cities every year after college graduation.

These facts are basically uncontested. But in general it's hard separate myth from [whatever isn't myth] about method acting, which was infused with self-mythology from the beginning. Clurman's memoir of the Group Theatre era is called *The Fervent Years*; all that fervency is impressive, but it can be tiresome to read about. The truth is that as I went about my research on method acting, I started to resent everyone involved for the same reason I resent the baby boomers: so much promise, and look at what you did with it. Fuck the twentieth century.

When the Group Theatre broke up at the end of the 1930s, the members mostly scattered, and some, like Stella Adler and Sanford Meisner, set up their own acting schools, with their own interpretations of Stanislavsky. Then, in 1947, Elia Kazan and Robert Lewis, also former Group members, decided to start the Actors Studio. According to Kazan, the idea was to give unemployed actors something to do instead of hanging out at drug stores all day. In any case, it became cool very quickly. And exclusive. You had to audition to get in and lots of people were turned down. As Kazan got busier in Hollywood and less interested in the workings of the Studio, he decided to bring Strasberg on as a teacher; in 1951, Strasberg became the Studio's artistic director.

Strasberg's version of Stanislavskian acting differs substantially from the others. Arguably, though, what really sets him apart is the aura of the Actors Studio under his directorship, from the mid-1950s to the mid-1970s, with its secrecy and hermeticism, its high concentration of movie stars, and the intensely psychological exercises of what came to be called the Method.

THE STORM HAD ended by the next morning. Josh walked me to a car rental where they gave me driving directions to Madison. I was so worried about taking a wrong turn that I kept the radio silent the whole way. The Wisconsin Historical Society is housed in an imposing building on the east end of the University of Wisconsin campus, with a long row of ionic columns embedded in the facade. I took an elevator up to the fourth floor to the Center for Film and Theater Research, where the archivists expected me. I had requested five tapes, three tagged “Affective Memory Exercise.” Not including the librarians, there were four other people in the room, which was brightly lit, with furniture that looked about thirty years old. The archivist reminded me that I could manually copy down whatever I liked, but that no recordings of any kind could be made of the materials. I assured him of my compliance.

It's not clear how or why the author of *The Gals and Guys of Beverly Hills, 90210* decided that Luke Perry used the affective memory exercise to portray Dylan McKay, but it may have something to do with the similarity between Perry's character and the star image of James Dean, an Actors Studio member from 1951 until his death in 1955. Dean's emotional performances are an iconic example of method acting, and the image of the brooding, leather-jacketed, "rebel without a cause" is indelibly linked to the Actors Studio. In Dean, the new celebrity imperative that a star's screen persona match his authentic self coincided with the Method's use of the actor's inner life. As one of his biographers wrote, "James Dean's identification with his characters was total. The density of link between motivation and action was complete. And self-incorporation and implicit identification became precisely the criteria for the new star."[1]

I was one of those teenagers with a poster of James Dean on her wall. Like everyone else, I was attracted to the pose of opposition. The idea that the actor stands apart from society, exiled from normal life and uniquely qualified to judge and condemn it, is an old one, but the sense that he incarnates a specifically psychic turmoil does seem to have developed around the middle of the twentieth century. What I experienced as a private passion has historical sources: the invention of the teenager as a marketing demographic, postwar ideas about art and authenticity, and the rise of method acting, which broadcast its iconography to the world through Hollywood films.

1 David Dalton, *James Dean, The Mutant King: A Biography* (Chicago: A Cappella Books, 2001), introduction.

THE VOICE OF Lee Strasberg is anxious and strained. He repeats himself and digresses at length, and his verbal tics are ubiquitous: "so to say," "as indicated by," "the result of which." It's the voice and the speech pattern of someone trying to communicate something important, but as I listened to the audio tapes, it felt to me that somehow the content had gone missing, or been transformed into a familiar-sounding but indecipherable dialect. There were long stretches that made close to no sense to me, exegeses of plays I'd never heard of, long iterations of the same instructions to multiple actors that sounded both epiphanic and strangely blank. I was most interested in what Strasberg had to say about emotional experience, so I listened hardest during those sections. This is because I had a hunch that for all his talk about truth and authenticity, for all the language of humanism, his method actually pointed in a different direction: towards a cyborg emotionality, a machinic self, fired with the blowtorch of mysticism.

When most people think of method acting, they think of movie stars who live their roles. They remember the story about Dustin Hoffman and Laurence Olivier on the set of *Marathon Man*, Hoffman barely sleeping and running until he collapsed to mirror the experience of his character, Olivier quipping, "you should try acting, my boy."

They might think of Val Kilmer, and the interview that almost ended his career:

> I anticipated that he might seem a little odd when we talked about acting, mostly because a) Kilmer is a Method actor, and b) all Method actors are insane. However, I did not realize how much insanity this process truly required.
>
> —You understand how it feels to shoot someone as much as a person who has actually committed a murder?
>
> —I understand it more. It's an actor's job. A guy who's lived through the horror of Vietnam has not spent his life preparing his mind for it... But this is what an actor trains to do. I can more effectively represent that kid in Vietnam than a guy who was there.
>
> —I don't question that you can more effectively represent it, but that's not the same thing. If you were talking to someone who's in prison for murder and the guy said, "Man, it really fucks you up to kill another person," do you think you could reasonably say, "I completely know what you're talking about"?
>
> —Oh yeah. I'd know what he's talking about.[2]

---

2 Chuck Klosterman, "Crazy Things Seem Normal...Normal Things Seem Crazy," *Chuck Klosterman IV: A Decade of Curious People and Dangerous Ideas* (Scribner, 2007), 38.

Going to acting school had been the best way I could think of to get to New York without completely alienating my school-teacher parents. But once there, I imagined myself sui generis. I remember telling someone, in all seriousness, that I wanted "to be an art object." I'm not sure what I thought I meant by that at the time, but I can see now what I did mean: it was a fantasy of enclosure. I wanted to be a thing. Jean-Paul Sartre would call this bad faith. Jacques Lacan would it call it the "armour of alienating identity." Simone de Beauvoir would call it identifying with the patriarchy. I think it was all of the above.

In my acting classes at Tisch, I was often reticent to participate. Anytime I had to get up in front of the class, though, I became focused. One of our first assignments was to write a monologue for ourselves about our lives. I had a hangover the day I had to present it, and had just bleached my hair in the dorm bathroom. Perversely, the teacher had pulled back the curtain from the mirrored wall of the classroom, so that we could watch ourselves acting; I can still picture my eighteen-year-old self with straw hair, pinching my eyes and crying.

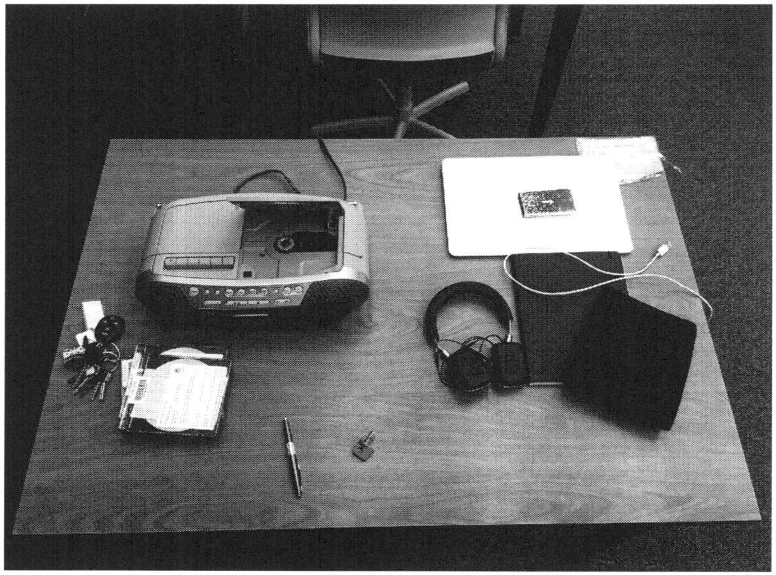

FROM THE TAPE recordings of Strasberg at the Actors Studio, you might be forgiven for thinking that there was remarkably little acting going on there. To make the tapes, the microphone had obviously been placed next to Strasberg, so the actors' voices are almost never audible, and when you do hear them, they're muted and indistinct, like they're speaking underwater. But the atmosphere feels prickly even so. One of the dialogues I transcribed was a conversation between Lee and an actress named Pat Randall:

PAT: I don't know, I couldn't laugh! I didn't have the freedom that I'd had before ... at the end usually I'm laughing.

STRASBERG: What do you mean usually—in these rehearsals?

PAT: *(overlapping)* I pick things that make me laugh.

STRASBERG: You mean usually in these rehearsals?

PAT: Yes.

STRASBERG: Or in life or when?

PAT: In life too! Whenever I'm drinking—one drink and I giggle all over the place.

STRASBERG: But you didn't drink now.

PAT: Oh no, I didn't!

STRASBERG: So therefore how could you giggle?

PAT: *(loud, shrill)* But that's what I want to do! I want to be able to do that and you can do it because I did it all during rehearsal and I didn't drink so why can't I do it in front of these people! That *(inaudible)*.

STRASBERG: You tell me.

PAT: Alright. So—

(Other voices, mostly male, laughing.)

STRASBERG: Don't laugh.

PAT: I know. *(More laughing, Pat and others. Pat screams, something inaudible)* I'VE STAYED UP UNTIL THREE IN THE MORNING LAUGHING! JUST TRYING IT OUT!

AND IT WORKS! *(something inaudible)* That's what I want to do this, do it every night!

STRASBERG: So you're not going to stay up until 3 o'clock in the morning doing it.

PAT: Oh Lee.

STRASBERG: You'll do it in performance.

PAT: You know what I mean.

STRASBERG: STOP LAUGHING! *(She isn't laughing; when he says that, she starts.)* STOP—DON'T LAUGH!

PAT: So anyway *(laughing)* we had this time and—

STRASBERG:—you see in other words you used the wrong principle. You stay up until 3 o'clock and you tell yourself to laugh, you're not going to laugh.

PAT: *(Shrill)* I KNOW that!

STRASBERG: If you tell yourself, don't laugh, you're going to laugh. *(Laughter)* Stop it!

PAT: *(laughing and maybe crying, maybe stamps her foot)* I don't feel anything and it worked so beautifully and I get up there and it goes right out the window! Now—that's technique, isn't it.

STRASBERG: No.

PAT: WHAT IS IT! It's being able to do it EVERY TIME!

STRASBERG: That's right.

PAT: All right.

STRASBERG: That's anticipation.

(Silence, then everyone in the room laughs.)

STRASBERG: I told you not to laugh, you see? In other words if you are prepared with the thing that leads to laughter but you feel you've got to laugh you will not laugh. I mean life does not like to be fooled. In life we often have impulses and feelings but if we're afraid as to what the other person

> is going to do about it we don't show them and we don't permit ourselves those feelings. Because we're afraid to be hurt and we're afraid—don't insult me. In life—life does not like to be fooled.

"The illusion of the first time" is the title of a book by the nineteenth-century actor William Gillette, and it became one of method acting's slogans. This is what Strasberg and Pat Randall are talking about: trying to behave with the illusion of spontaneity, as though she hasn't been staying up till 3 AM to repeat the same thing over and over. It's a common theme in the audio recordings. Actors, frustrated with the impossibility of repeating without repetition, bang their heads against the immovable wall of Strasberg's certainty. Life does not like to be fooled.

Method acting transforms what was once understood to be spontaneous in acting, the product of inspiration, into something technical, repeatable, methodical. As Strasberg put it, "we try to take the mystery out of acting in the sense that we try to give to acting a craft."[3] But Pat's aggravation doesn't evoke a failure of technique so much as a kind of bereavement: the realization that the performance has died, and can't be revived.

3 Lee Strasberg, *Strasberg at the Actors Studio: The Tape-Recorded Sessions*, ed. Robert H. Hethmon (New York: Theatre Communications Group, 1993), 241.

Strasberg's exercises can be divided into two basic categories. The first is devoted to relaxation. Strasberg is convinced that human beings are "blocked," that this blockage stems from social and cultural conditioning, and that unblocking the actor is the first step towards authentic emotional expression. The second group of exercises is devoted to its own form of conditioning: conditioning the actor to respond to fictional sensory and emotional material as he or she would to real sensory and emotional material. Here is where things get tricky. The actor practices what is called affective memory, which includes both sense memory and emotional memory exercises, to train her to respond to stimuli on stage in a truthful and authentic way. She imagines she is holding a "breakfast drink" and practices smelling and tasting it. She also practices emotional recall, summoning up emotional memories from her past and reliving them. The internal sequence of the emotional memory exercise changed somewhat over the course of Strasberg's career, but it always started with the actor narrating the emotional event from her past sensorially (what she saw, what sounds she heard, what textures she felt) and then re-enacting the event without narrating it. After the actor has practiced this many times, she should be able to summon up the real emotion she felt in her past at will while she's performing.

The emotional memory exercise is the most famous and controversial of Strasberg's exercises, and the crux of the criticism that he was practicing unlicensed psychotherapy. At the Historical Society, I listened to tape recordings of several affective memory exercises, taking notes on my laptop. This from a tape marked "Anna Stanovich (1966, April 19)":

> Long pause on the tape (from 28:12 to 29:15).
>
> We just hear her breathing. Then she screams ("uggghghhhhh!!!"), almost as if disgusted, or frustrated, and then sobs several times. Then silence. Sobs again at 30:06.

Continues sobbing, and maybe laughing, sobbing louder ("ahhhhrrrrgghhh"!) Says something: "all right"?

"I wish from that ... [inaudible] ..."

Another two minutes of silence. Moving around the room? Sighs.

Another five minutes of silence.

Then—Strasberg says "that's it? Now had you intended to do more? Why didn't you?"

Anna says something inaudible.

"You got very frightened of what?"

Pause.

ANNA: "I don't know. I don't know what happened. I just got very frightened at one point."

I LEFT THE archives that night before it closed. I was tired of listening to Strasberg berate actors and monologue about nothing. His voice had started blurring in my head with the voice of my grandfather, a psychiatrist and a controlling and narcissistic person. When I started doing the research for my dissertation on method acting, in my third year of graduate school, it seemed like a perfect way to use an otherwise wasted chapter of my life. But during the six years or so of working on it, I often felt like one of the Studio actors on the tape recordings: uncertain, resentful, desperate for approval, and terrified by the specter of annihilation lurking around every turn.

I tried to go to bed early, but tossed and turned for hours. I wondered if I had food poisoning. I half-hallucinated that I was stuck in Madison forever, trudging endlessly to the archives, imprisoned with the voices of the vengeful midcentury, slowly turning into something—maybe a pillar of salt.

STRASBERG WAS BORN in a small village in Austrian Poland, now Ukraine, in 1901. His family emigrated to New York, and he grew up on the Lower East Side, where he had small roles in the then-thriving Yiddish theater. He recalled that world in his autobiography, *A Dream of Passion*. Surprisingly for someone who believed that "the experiences which a human being has gone through are literally engraved into the fiber into the network of nervous system," Strasberg's memories are riddled with absences.[4] "I have no recollection of what happened on stage," he writes of his first experience performing, "I did not carry away any observations or anecdotes ... I remember the rehearsals only in the sense that I remember there were rehearsals."[5] One of the only memories he retained was a lecture given by the principal of his Hebrew school, who was also the head of the Progressive Dramatic Club: "He was a strange, peasant-like man with a body and face that seemed carved out of clay," Strasberg recounts, "he lectured to us about the history of Jewish drama, stressing its folk roots, its earthiness, and its sense of realistic characterization. It was as if one of the granite Egyptian statues was talking with a haunting, unchanging intensity."[6]

It's easy to see the connection between this description and Strasberg's aesthetic interests: "realistic characterization" is the goal of method acting, and "earthy" is one of Strasberg's favorite words to describe the kind of acting he likes. What's more interesting is the imagery that Strasberg uses to evoke the Hebrew school principal's vehemence. The "strange, peasant-like man" with a "body and face carved out of clay" or "granite," as "haunting, unchanging" as a statue—this is an image of the golem.

The golem is a mythical creature from medieval Judaism, an anthropomorphic monster made out of clay and brought it to life in

4 UCD 339/A62 (2 of 2) UCD Box 26, Actors Studio Collection, Wisconsin Historical Society.

5 Lee Strasberg, *A Dream of Passion: The Development of the Method* (New York: Plume, 1988), 9.

6 Ibid., 11.

an ecstatic ritual. According to some legends, the golem is awakened when the rabbi-creator stamps the Hebrew word for truth (*emet*) on its forehead and destroyed when the first letter is removed: *met* means death. As a monster, the golem in some ways prefigures Frankenstein's: the "body without a soul," the dead matter enlivened and let loose on the world. It could also be figure for the method actor, in whom the archaic past is awakened to embody the violence of the Word.

POWER
MODE
TAPE
CD
RADIO BAND
AUDIO IN
SONY

I SPENT THE rest of the night violently throwing up in the bathroom. Getting sick by yourself in a hotel room in an unfamiliar city is an existentially rich experience. Deprived of the opportunity to theatricalize my feebleness for an audience, I could focus on nothing but the gross substances of my usually coddled body. In my feverish self-aggrandizement, I started to feel exalted, as if vomiting the contents of my stomach somehow got me closer to the pit of my bare life. The entire trip had been somewhat masochistic from the beginning; this felt like a literalization of the abjection that, in other forms, I'd secretly loved the most about acting. It was obvious that Lee Strasberg was cursing me from beyond the grave.

THERE'S ANOTHER STRANGE thing about Strasberg's memory of his Hebrew school principal: his comparison of him to an Egyptian statue in particular. I myself am the daughter of a Hebrew school principal, and I can tell you that it's truly bizarre to compare one to an Egyptian. Perhaps the most important story in the Jewish tradition, the story of Passover, involves the flight of the Jews from their Egyptian slave-drivers. But Strasberg's substitution of the Egyptian overlord for the Jewish peasant says something about the traumatized assimilationist longings of Jews in the postwar era. There's much in Strasberg's writing, and the writing about him, that speaks to that anxious conformism: the social climbing, the needy authoritarianism, the affected worldliness, the reverence for intellectual advancement.

The Jewishness of method acting is usually noted only in passing. From one angle, this is an odd omission: Clurman, Strasberg, Adler, Meisner were all Jewish. However, whatever is ethnically and culturally specific about their acting methods is not easy to discern in their writings, with their ubiquitous references to universal values, universal emotions, universal psychology. In fact, without that universalism, the basic tenets of method acting fall apart: how can you use your own emotional experiences as fodder for your character's if all human lives are not basically the same?

When I wrote a bit about method acting's repressed Jewishness in my dissertation, my advisor got really excited. "You should title this section, 'Call Me Shoshana,'" he said. I ended up cutting most of it out of the final manuscript. I don't know why; maybe he touched a nerve. It's true that the closer my research came to my own experience the more I felt sucked into the Method's orbit, rotating around its sun of self-exposure on the axes of eros/disgust.

THERE ARE TWO main narratives about Strasberg and method acting. The first is summed up by Louis Scheeder: "Lee Strasberg transformed Russian theatrical practice into a symbol of American freedom and nationalism."[7] The second belongs to feminist criticism, like Sue-Ellen Case's *Feminism and Theater*: "the psychological construction of character ... places the female actor within the range of systems that have oppressed her."[8] These are two versions of the same story: method acting is about nationalism, chauvinism, the patriarchy.

The Method I was interested in was something different. The gothic exorcisms of the emotional memory exercise, the traumatized *Yiddishkeit* of Strasberg's meandering speeches, the ferociousness of actors like Joanne Woodward and Geraldine Page. And the strung-out melancholy of the Actors Studio, which started to seem like the place you go after your dreams have died. The story I read about again and again from Studio actors is of waking up the morning after their brilliant successes, champagne still wet on their lips, and discovering that they feel empty, frightened, and alone. The Studio picks you up at the moment of disillusionment; it catches you leaning over the abyss. You go there the morning after. But what happens the morning after that?

7 Louis Scheeder, "Strasberg's Method and the Ascendency of American Acting," *Training of the American Actor*, ed. Arthur Bartow (New York: Theatre Communications Group, 2006), 3.

8 Sue-Ellen Case, *Feminism and Theater* (New York: Routledge, 1988), 122.

BY 6 AM, there was nothing left in my stomach and it was late enough in New York to call Michael. My return flight was at 7 PM, and before then I had to return the car to Chicago. The thought of staying another day and night in Madison was too horrible to seriously contemplate. So I got up, took a shower, and found a drugstore where I bought ginger ale and an assortment of anti-nausea medications. Then, strung out and severely dehydrated, I got back in the car just as it started to rain. I could barely see anything through the storm, and had to pull over twice to stop the pounding in my head. When my phone rang with an unfamiliar number, I ignored it, then thought of the canceled flight on the way in and listened to the message. Gripping the steering wheel with one hand, and wondering about the cell phone laws on the Wisconsin highway system, I listened to the message from American Airlines telling me my flight had been canceled and that the only other flight to New York that night left two hours earlier than the other, two and a half hours from the time of the call. My GPS said it would take me an hour and a half to get to Chicago. I called back and said I would take it, and drove extremely fast, thinking I might die on the highway, but I was definitely going to get out of Wisconsin.

I got to the car rental and threw the keys at the guy behind the desk, demanding to know the fastest way to the airport. He pointed down the block to the L. The subway station was on the other side of a freeway overpass, under which a dozen or so homeless people had camped. I got on the train breathless, glaring, and got to the airport, where they let me jump the security line. I ran to my gate. The flight had been canceled.

I ended up staying another night in Chicago at a Holiday Inn Express by the airport. The airline only paid for half the room, but I was too demoralized to feel indignant. In the hallway leading to my room on the eleventh floor, a door opened and I saw two children crying on one of the beds. The bar in the lobby was full of glassy-eyed couples and exhausted workers. Feeling hideous and feral, I ordered a burger, and briskly threw it up in the bathroom.

Something happened to Strasberg at the Actors Studio. The tendencies that Clurman noticed during their Group Theatre days—Strasberg's "fanatic[ism] on the subject of true emotion," which he "sought with the patience of an inquisitor," the fact that "the adoration of the actors for Lee Strasberg seemed to have the effect of inflating his ego with what struck me as a sense of total mastery"[9]—mushroomed into an insistence on total self-revelation; the Method started to look less like art and more like one of the self-actualization cults and near-cults that proliferated in New York and LA in the 1960s and 1970s. Herbert Blau in 1982 described the "private moment" exercise, another of Strasberg's core techniques, in which actors present a scene of themselves alone, as an activity "at the brink of transgression or taboo":

> The extremity of the Private Moment for the Method actor (with Brando as the archetype) was—for maximum truth of emotion, insensibly there—the moment of an almost unspeakable, maybe illicit incitation, at the brink of transgression or taboo, like a rape that has never been confessed or breaking the incest barrier or some actual or desired self-mutilation—what in the repertoire of postmodern sexuality is being played out in S&M or B&D.[10]

You can hear rumblings of this on the tape recordings, in the actors' spikes of rage and shame. It's easy to imagine them spilling their guts at EST meetings, getting naked at meditation centers, going on vision quests to India, locking themselves in hotel rooms with bad drugs. Brando wasn't a student of Strasberg's, but he was

9 Harold Clurman, *The Fervent Years: The Group Theatre and the Thirties* (New York: Da Capo, 1983), 44, 51.

10 Herbert Blau, "Deep Throat: The Grail of the Voice," *The Dubious Spectacle: Extremities of Theater, 1976–2000* (Minneapolis: University of Minnesota, 2002), 121.

an early member of the Actors Studio, and remains, as Blau puts it, "the archetype." And his own trajectory, from iconoclastic but bankable movie star to the caricature he embodied by the 1980s, tracks the messiness of the long tail of the Method.

By the 1970s, method acting had become baroque. It had also become an ethos of filmmaking. When Blau mentioned Brando in 1982, the actor's major recent role was Colonel Kurtz in *Apocalypse Now*, a film described by its director, Francis Ford Coppola, as "not a movie. My film is not about Vietnam; it is Vietnam."[11] Life would no longer be fooled.

11 *Hearts of Darkness: A Filmmaker's Apocalypse*, directed by Fax Bahr and George Hickenlooper (1991; American Zoetrope Studios), DVD. Stella Adler, *The Art of Acting* (New York: Applause Books, 2000), 66.

89118281252
b89118281252a
UCD 339A/190 (2 of 2) (UCD Box 17)
The Actors Studio
Actors Unit 190 6/1962
Track One: Comments by Lee Strasberg, continued from a prior tape (339A/189?) 59:10
WISCONSIN HISTORICAL SOCIETY
89118281567
b89118281567a
Researcher's Name (Please
UCD 339A/190 (1 of 2) (UCD Box 17)
The Actors Studio
Actors Unit 190 6/1962
Track One: "Natural Affection" by Bill Hyde with Shelley Winters and Chris Jones, 6/8/1962 50:56
Track Two: "Henry IV", part 1 with Rip Torn and Walter Beakel, 6/8/1962 13:46
RESTRICTED
RESTRICTION: Onsite listening use only. No sale or off-site use by patrons.
This audio may not be copied, quoted beyond Fair Use, published or broadcast without written permission
WISCONSIN HISTORICAL SOCIETY

One of the tape-recorded Actors Studio sessions that Robert Hethmon included in his edited volume includes a conversation between Strasberg, several actors, and a "young playwright," who, in an atypical fit of forthrightness, challenges Strasberg's approach:

> YOUNG PLAYWRIGHT: The question was made necessary for me by what had happened that day, but the same thing had happened before almost every time I have been to the Studio. I feel very uncomfortable, and I feel it is unnecessary for someone after a scene to discuss his personal problems as an actor ... To expose himself, and to discuss these problems openly is embarrassing, and I think it's fruitless.
> STRASBERG: There must always be special knowledge in approaching any kind of theatre work on a technical level, that is, where the audience is excluded and the people who watch are part of the workers.
> YOUNG PLAYWRIGHT: I dislike being put into an attitude of sympathy toward the actor.
> STRASBERG: If someone watches an operation and faints away, is it the fault of the doctor? I'm sorry. You go to a theatre to see plays. Here you're seeing operations on plays! If this work was brought to you on a public platform, we would leave ourselves open to your kind of judgment. Here it's different ...
> ACTOR D: It took me about two years of asking the wrong questions and being slapped down to train myself to look and listen and try to understand. No actor ever does any work without involving his personal problems. For instance, I was working in a Broadway show once where the director made us play with such intensity that I was tied up in knots. I had to find out whether it was possible for me to relax as an actor again. I chose a scene and brought it to the Studio

> and said I only wanted to relax. This would probably not have embarrassed you, but it was quite personal to me. If you had observed longer, you would have noticed from time to time that an actor will start to explain something, and Lee will say, "Stop. That's getting too personal." We have in him a man who can decide.
>
> ACTRESS E: Some of us have watched one another four of five years, some of us ten years. If you waited a little, you would see that it did something. Here we are dealing with our careers. Maybe it does us good to get up and say, "How am I going to change this quality in myself?" Suppose people say to me, "All you're good for is neurotic parts." I don't want to tell people things about neurotic women the rest of my life. Suppose I want to tell things about lovely, happy women once in awhile? "Help me!" That's personal, and that is an actor's problem. That's what we're here for, and some of us have watched others of us beat the rap.
>
> ACTOR A: You must understand that when we come in here to work, it's to find a root. I come here for a specific, personal reason. I disagree with Lee Strasberg a lot of the time, but he represents a catalyst, a conscience, a way to work, a constant finger pointed at me. I've had a taste of this cup of success, and I must say it tastes kind of flat. I've been trying to find a way to flavor it. He knows the formula. That's why I come to the Studio.[12]

How am I going to change this quality in myself? There are numerous qualities about myself I'd like to change. Can you help me, Lee? It's impossible, on the one hand, not to feel superior to these credulous actors, going back to the Studio week after week, year

12 *Strasberg at the Actors Studio*, ed. Robert H. Hethmon, 47–49.

after year, failing to get roles and living out their unfulfilling lives. It's impossible not to be a little disgusted by the actors who crave being pointed at by Lee's paternalistic finger of judgment and not to sympathize with the "Young Playwright," who finds it all "very uncomfortable." On the other hand, it's also hard not to empathize with the actors' helplessness in the face of great, unfeeling forces, and their hunger to attach themselves to a man who "knows the formula," "a man who can decide." What's hard for me to understand isn't the sentiment, it's the lack of self-consciousness in these actors who so baldly declare their needs.

In the opening sequence of *Apocalypse Now*, we find Martin Sheen red and sweaty, passed out next to a bottle of Scotch and a heroin spoon, as the noise of helicopters becomes the noise of the overhead fan in the Saigon hotel room where Captain Willard is waiting for his next mission. He does iffy martial arts in his underwear; smashes the mirror with his fist, cutting his hand; somersaults over the bed; smears his face with the blood from his hand; guzzles booze; and finally collapses, naked and tangled in the bloody bed sheets, into open-mouthed sobs. Sheen reported later that when they filmed this scene he was "so drunk [he] couldn't stand up," and actually did cut his hand on the mirror. "I just went very deep into my own personal pain, and alcoholism, and self-loathing, and all the things that make up a human being," he said. "I just showed a completely broken, desperate guy, which was a reflection pretty much of who I was at the time."

In contrast, Brando seems tame, professorial, an emissary from an earlier era, an era of monologues, scene studies, improvisation exercises. He speaks precisely, calmly, through his teeth. He pats water on his face almost delicately. Sheen is the one exposed. When Willard is told that his mission will entail the termination of a Green Beret colonel, he is informed that the colonel's methods have become "unsound." But what had become unsound was the Method itself, its tenuous center erupted, its subtexts bleeding all over the screen.

Later, after Willard has seen what's become of Kurtz, now the ruler of an army of "natives" who "worship him like a god," Kurtz asks Willard whether he thinks his methods have become unsound. Willard replies, "I don't see any method at all, Sir."

I WAS BORN at the end of the twentieth century. I turned seventeen in the year 2000. Here's an emotional memory: the first summer of the new millennium, I drove with some friends from Berkeley up to Humboldt county for the memorial service of the semi-estranged father of one of our classmates, a Vietnam veteran, who'd died of cancer someone told me was from exposure to Agent Orange. The family owned a rambling property in the hills that he'd turned into a marijuana farm, and when we got there, everyone was out back behind the house, pitching tents and smoking. Maria's dad had eight or nine children from various relationships, and they were all gorgeous, auburn and large. His memorial service was made up of spontaneous verse recitations, burning sage, and a dubious Native American ritual; his group of friends and girlfriends, though mostly gray and droopy, had put on their beads and belts and braided their hair, and stood around hugging the giant children and swaying arm-in-arm. I met an angel-faced teenager named Tommy, the blond son of the property's caretaker. I remember the smoke from the end of the campfire and the rocky ground in the yard by the porch. It was a fantasy come true. It was a movie from the '70s.

No: it was a movie from the year 2000 about the '70s; a pirated experience, party-crashing other people's loss. The Vietnam War was exotic to me, even romantic; I was in the California of a Hollywood imagination. I was blithe, I was high, I could play '70s for a night, no problem. The detritus of the twentieth century was there for that, beginning with the most saccharine clichés and ending with the death of the last and only Vietnam vet I knew.

What strikes me now is not the superficiality of it, or even the cliché, but how well I played that role. I knew I was repeating. I tried to do it well—tried to do it, I mean, with the "illusion of the first time." And I have a hunch that many other people around my age have approximately the same memory: that night it could have almost been the '70s, as long as you ignored the dead.

I GOT BACK to New York around noon and got into bed. It was a bright, hot day, and the curtains in the bedroom glowed. When I try to imagine what it must have been like to be a member of the Actors Studio in the '70s, I picture the end of a session, when the actors pick up their things to go home. I picture a woman with fluffy hair and lines on her face, lifting her sweater from the back of her chair and responding to a man who asks a bit too pointedly what she's been doing. Oh, you know, she says, I've been working with a theater company on a one-act, no money but someone knows a producer, so we'll see. Or: I just had an audition for a cold cream commercial, but I don't think I'll get it. Or: I'm doing soaps, it's good for now, and I think next year I'll have a speaking role. For many cultural critics today, the actor is emblematic of American post-Fordist work culture that since the '70s has impressed itself on our subjectivity with greater and greater force: the requirement that you fully embody and wholeheartedly commit to each and every role, despite constantly shuffling between different bad jobs; the omnipresent insecurity; the perpetual fear of falling out, getting left behind, being forgotten. I live in a situation of relative comfort and stability, protected by a university and many other privileges, but there was terror when I lay in bed that week after my trip to Madison, cocooned in frustration and shame.

SANTA MONICA
7900 W
LEE STRASBERG THEATRE
ILM INSTITUTE
WEST HOLLYWOOD - NEW
HEILMAN

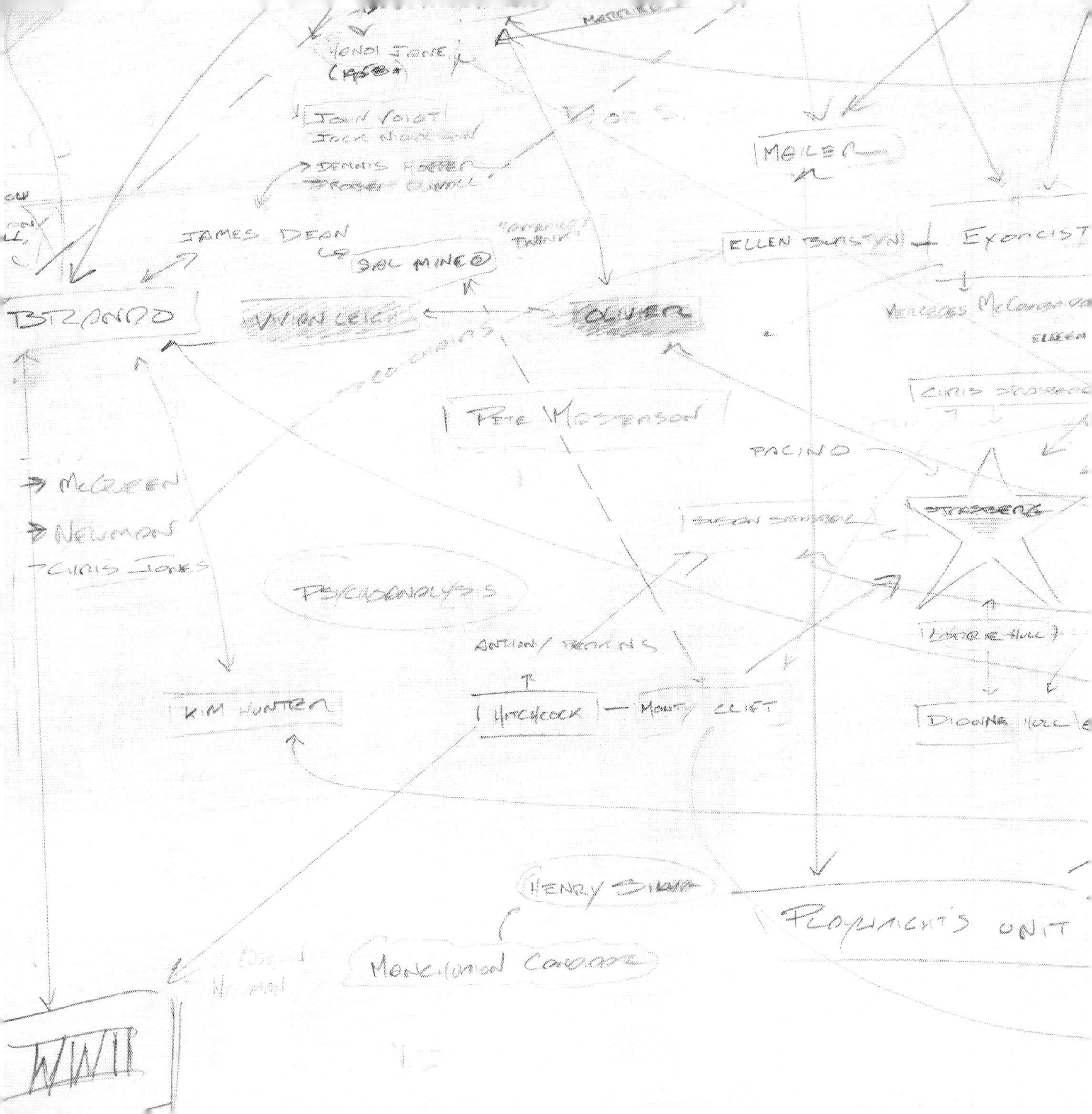

HONDI JONE (1958*)
JOHN VOIGT
JACK NICHOLSON
DENNIS HOPPER
ROBERT DUVALL
D. OF S.
MEILER
JAMES DEAN
SAL MINEO
"AMERICA'S TWINK"
ELLEN BURSTYN
EXORCIST
BRANDO
VIVIAN LEIGH
OLIVIER
CO-STARS
CHRIS STRASBERG
PETE MOSTERSON
PACINO
McQUEEN
NEWMAN
CHRIS JONES
SUSAN STRASBERG
STRASBERG
PSYCHOANALYSIS
ANTHONY PERKINS
LORRIE HULL
KIM HUNTER
HITCHCOCK
MONTY CLIFT
DIONNE HULL
HENRY SILVA
PLAYWRIGHT'S UNIT
MANCHURIAN CANDIDATE
WWII

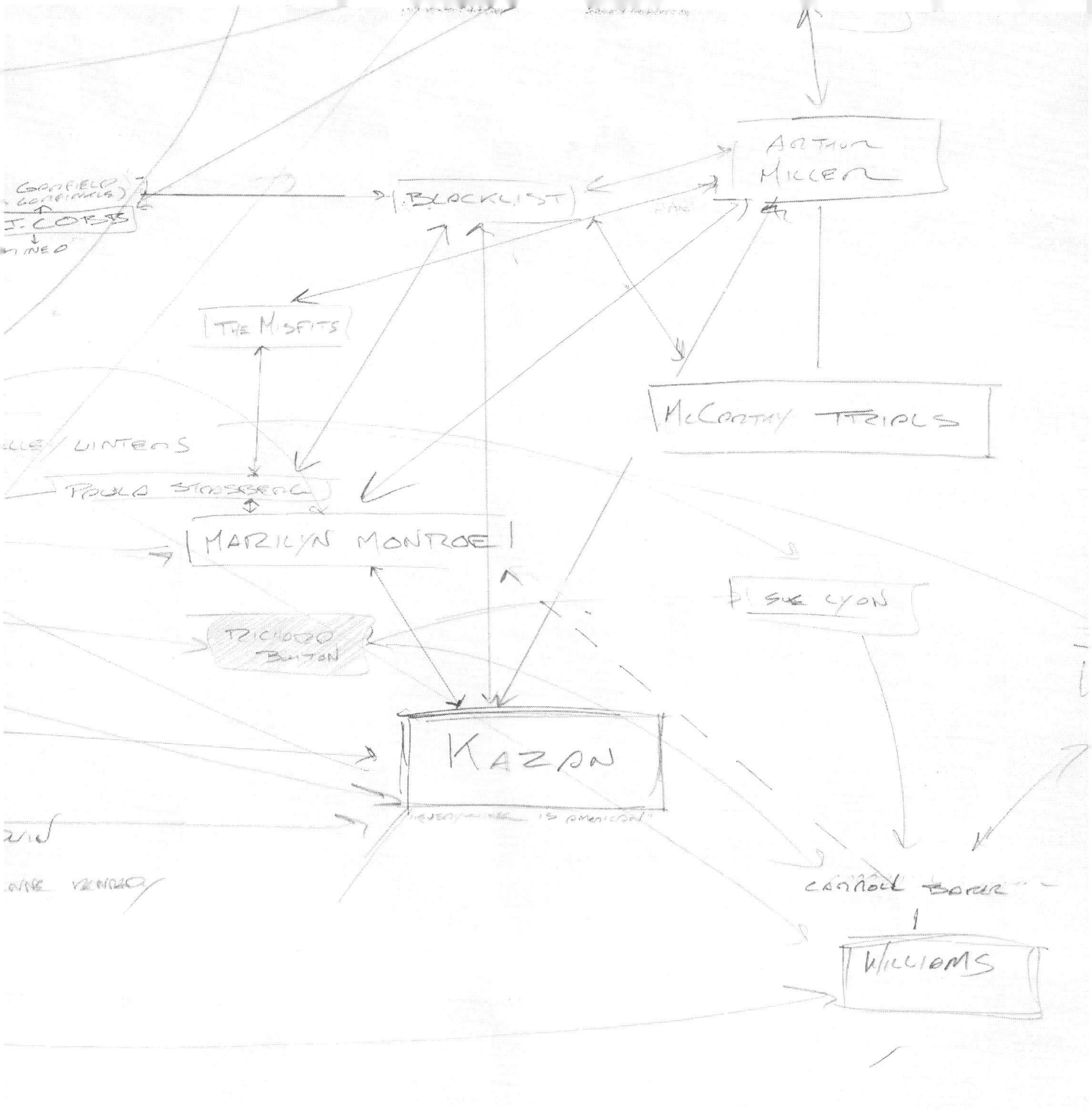

ARTHUR MILLER
J. COBB
BLACKLIST
THE MISFITS
McCARTHY TRIALS
PAULA STRASBERG
MARILYN MONROE
RICHARD BURTON
SUE LYON
KAZAN
CARROLL BAKER
WILLIAMS

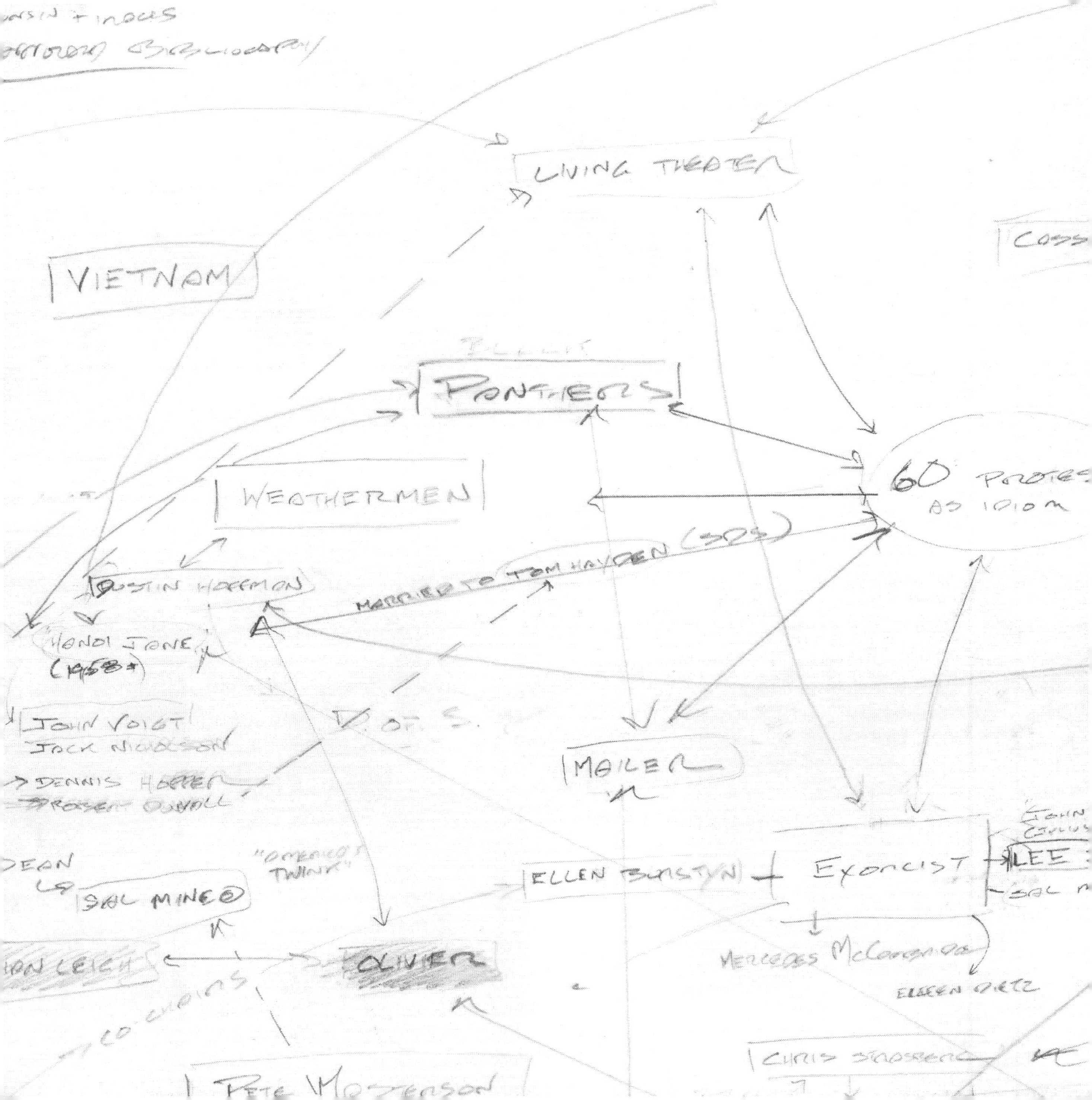
LIVING THEATER
VIETNAM
PANTHERS
WEATHERMEN
60 PROTES
AS IDIOM
MARRIED TO TOM HAYDEN (SDS)
DUSTIN HOFFMAN
"HANOI JANE"
JOHN VOIGT
JACK NICHOLSON
DENNIS HOPPER
ROBERT DUVALL
D. OF S.
MAILER
"AMERICA'S TWINK"
SAL MINEO
ELLEN BURSTYN
EXORCIST
LEE
MERCEDES McCAMBRIDGE
EILEEN DIETZ
OLIVER
CO-CHAIRS
PETE MASTERSON

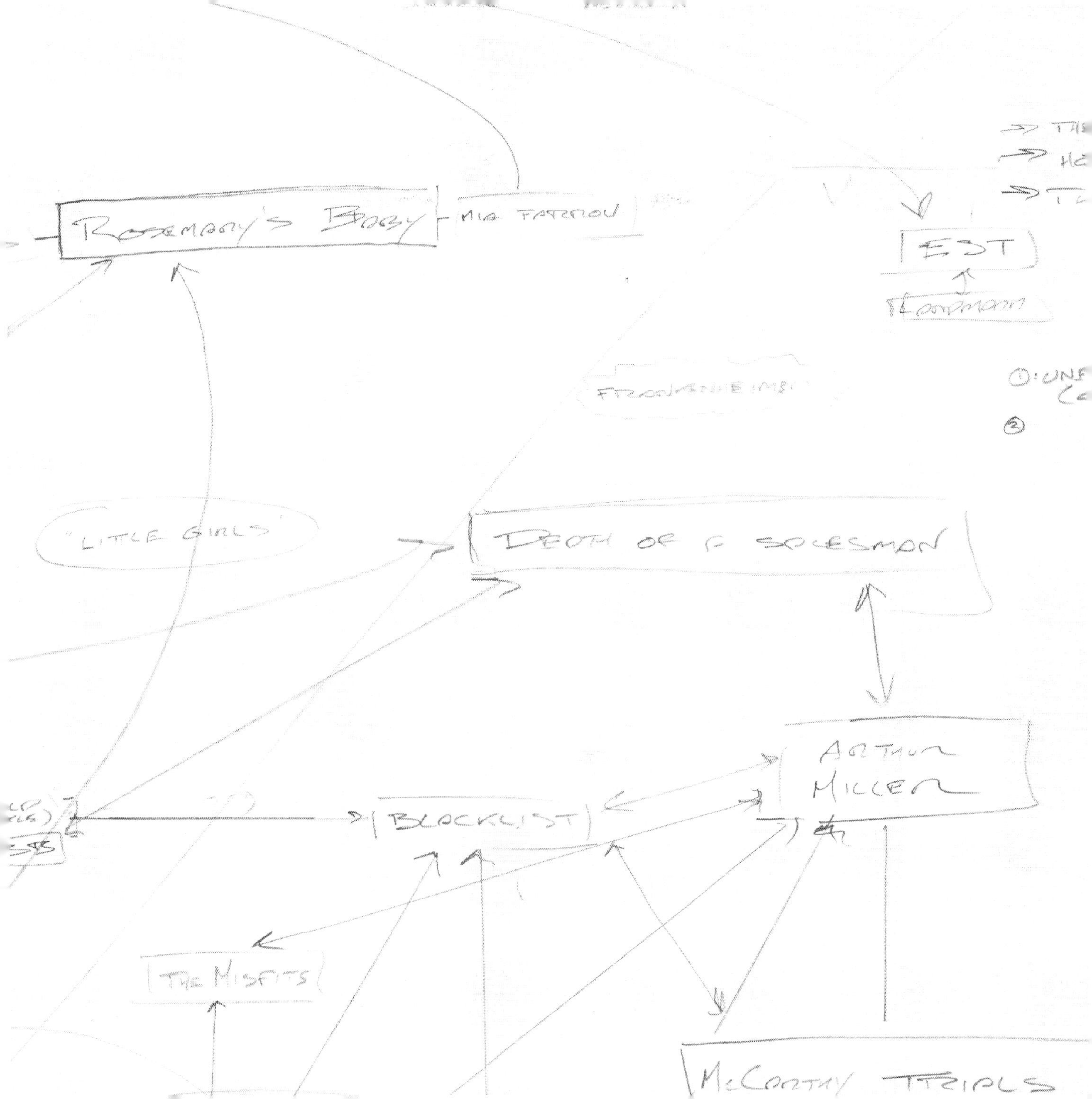

ROSEMARY'S BABY
MIA FARROW
EST
"LITTLE GIRLS"
DEATH OF A SALESMAN
ARTHUR MILLER
BLACKLIST
THE MISFITS
McCARTHY TRIALS

Edition of Eight

David Levine

An exhibition space. There are seven large, framed black-and-white photos on the wall. At the center of the room is a white plinth with nothing on it. Beside the plinth, on the floor, is a mask of a robot's face. VOX approaches a gallery visitor as a gallery visitor.

VOX:

Excuse me—

Do you know what this is?

Indicates robot mask on the floor, next to plinth.

Do you know why it's not *on* the plinth? Like, what that's supposed to mean?

I mean, it seems like a pretty deliberate gesture—close enough to the plinth to remind you that it's not on the plinth? Is that … ?

I hate wall text because it distracts me from the art, but sometimes these gestures just seem arbitrary.

Maybe in the press release?

Like, big whoop. You put it next to instead of on the plinth. And this demonstrates … what? The destruction of Western art? Like no one's ever deconstructed exhibition rhetoric?

Looking around.

I wonder about conceptualism, sometimes. Or, I guess, post— … post-post-conceptualism. Conceptualism as it exists today. The idea that this stuff would be self-explanatory. Or: the idea that it *isn't* self-explanatory—"research-based practice"—and that the explanation is actually part of the work … that you need the background for the artwork to fully realize itself.

Except apparently they're hedging their bets, right? Because this stuff is displayed like it's a … Rothko. Or a Rosenquist. Or whatever. Self-contained. Autonomous. *Visual*. The press release is out front. The wall text—OK, in this case no wall text but you know what I mean—stays off to the side. As though it isn't part of the work. As though it's just supporting material. Like it's a question of decorum. Like, "Oh, you can contemplate this artwork in silence like a Pollock! But of course, this work is actually antagonistic to that entire legacy, so we do have this text here. But we wouldn't want to be prescriptive! Look how boldly the work bodies forth! Of *course* you can generate your own meanings! But not in that AbEx "what-do-you-see-in-it?" kind of way … Um, listen: you just contemplate, dear, and we'll just put the language over here, discretely, in case the rich network of references of which this image is merely a node doesn't just jump out at you."

Indicates an artwork.

Like, what do you think this *means*?

Or what's your experience of this? What explains ME? What is your experience of me?

It's like everyone's a little ashamed, even now, of needing an explanation or a conceptual apparatus. Or the conceptual apparatus is a little ashamed of itself—so it shies off to the side, whispering there, an éminence grise conspiring with the press release, both of them whispering to this dumb, brute object here, telling it what to *be*, filling it with lies.

These exhibition texts are lines of code, synchronizing an entire gallery's worth of things into behaving. It's like a smart kitchen. It's like possession. Have you ever seen *Demon Seed*?

Demon Seed is the story of an AI that becomes sentient, and eventually goes out of control. There were a lot of these movies, before *Blade Runner* and *Terminator*. It used to be: big dumb robots over here—Stepford Wives, Westworld, Fembots—and disembodied AIs—HAL 9000,WOPR, MUTHUR—over there.

And the thing about *Demon Seed*—which is a super-weird movie, and not, by the way, about demons—is that it tries to bridge this gap by having an AI—*Proteus*—take over a smart kitchen—actually a whole smart home—and then impregnate Julie Christie in it, um ... with it. And she winds up giving birth to the intense metallic baby of the title, which she learns to love and which initially looks exactly like a bad sculpture. But one thing you *can* say about it: it can certainly speak for itself.

Nudges mask with foot.

Can this thing speak for itself?

Apologetic.

Sorry. Not allowed to touch the art.

Vaults up onto the plinth.

Unless you're the art. Haha.

We had a moment there, though, right? At the beginning? When you thought I might be ... Right?

Sighs.

And now we're immune to each other. I'm ... a specimen of something. You're watching, I'm doing.

I just want a connection, you know?

This is a shitty space to make a connection in.

Vito Acconci used to do this thing. It was called *Proximity Piece*. And he did it—well, he only did it once—as far as we know!—at the Jewish Museum, in 1969, for a group show called *Software*. He would hang out in the galleries all day, and when he saw a patron looking at work he would just go up to them like he was looking at the work too, and just stand much too close to them. And then he would watch them silently freak out and leave the room in a huff. That was it. That was the piece. There's only like three photos. I always imagine him doing it to a little old lady in cats-eye glasses and a clear plastic rain bonnet, although I guess that's unlikely, huh?

I admire it. The humility of it, y'know? Acconci was kind of a masochist, but it's a very humble stance, right? Alienating your neighbors—making sure they think you're a freak, watching them physically shun you and resisting the temptation to be like, "An artwork by Tino Seghal, 2014." Just receiving all that hostility, accepting their hostility head on, without marking himself as a special artist. As far as they know he's just a gross, lank-haired perv. Not a specimen of a perv; not an artist who makes pervosity part of their practice; just a perv.

As far as they know. Because he's secretly Vito Acconci acting out a conceptual agenda, and he gets to hire the photographer who makes that lady in the cats-eye glasses look like a idiot for all

eternity in that *Candid Camera* way for the benefit of people like us—well, people like you—But: as far as they know, Adrian Piper was just a little black man walking around Harvard Square; Lynn Hershman Leeson was just another unmarried woman, dating and going to work and seeing a shrink; Tehching Hsieh was just another homeless guy. And the thing is, without that "ta-da!" moment, everyone's swimming through the same water—reality doesn't separate into … this.

I miss that.

There's this moment in *Invasion of the Body Snatchers*—the remake—that clarifies this really well: it's at the end, where Veronica Cartwright is trying to pass as an alien—a pod person—in a San Francisco now full of pod people, and she spots Donald Sutherland, and tries to connect with him thinking he's also a human but—surprise!—he's actually an alien and suddenly his eyes bulge and his mouth opens and he does that crazy sybillant thing the aliens do when they spot a human and he points his finger at her and suddenly they're all pointing and the world has gone from being a plane of fluid social interactions, where everyone's performing just hard enough to seem like they're not performing—to a world of audience and performer. One minute you're just being you, and the next minute you're stuck onstage, just because some fucker has decided to disengage and start pointing. That's us. That's you and me. You're Donald Sutherland.

But what about that guy over there? What about the person watching the video in the next room? What about the person running the gallery desk? Maybe they're part of the artwork too. Maybe we're a hive-mind. Maybe *we're* Donald Sutherland.

Quoting:

> “Tout le temps, je vois, et je revois,
> Tous ces gens qui se reconnaissent.
> Quelque chose passaient entre eux tous,
> Quelque secret.
>
> J’ai vécu toute ma vie dans cette
> ville, mais aujourd’hui
> J’ai eu le sentiment que toute
> avait changé.
>
> Les gens etaient differents.
> Pas seulement George, mais tout le monde.
> Hier tout semblait normal.
> Aujourd’hui tout semblait le même,
> Mais ne l’était pas.
>
> C’etait un cauchemar.
> C’est devenu effrayant.
> Comme si toute la ville avait changé
> Du jour au lendemain.”

You like that? It’s Baudelaire.

Nah, I’m fucking with you. It’s from the french dub of *Invasion of the Body Snatchers*.

Remember Acconci’s photographer. We could also be watching *you*.

Lifts arm, points at spectator, and does the Body Snatchers *shriek.*

It's always funny how those parts work. Like, you've got a robot pretending to be a human; or an alien pretending to be a human; or a demon pretending to be a human. So you hire an actor to pretend to be a robot pretending to be a human. And since the robot or alien or is supposed to be convincing, all a good actor needs to do is play the character the robot has to play; they don't even need to worry about playing a robot playing that character, because they're the robot, right? But as soon as something goes wrong, as soon as the robot malfunctions or the alien is discovered, the actor has to start doing all this extremely technical work with, like, alien yodeling or

Does the Paula Prentiss malfunction waltz from The Stepford Wives.

"I was just going to give you coffee. I thought we were friends. I was just going to give you coffee. I thought we were friends. I thought we were friends. I thought we were friends."

That was good, right?

It took me a while.

So basically, the less convincing the robot is, the more work I have to do to be convincingly a robot. Which is kind of bass-ackwards, right? Shouldn't I have to do less work to be less convincing? They should just hire a robot instead. I wouldn't feel exploited.

I always wanted to write this screenplay. This penguin-looking guy—short, white, ethnic—basically Richard Dreyfus or Al

Pacino or Dustin Hoffman or any of these guys who became stars in the early 70s—moves to New York to become an actor. He falls under the influence of Lee Strasberg, the inventor of Method Acting, at the Actor's Studio. Riots going on, Viet Nam, bombings, all that stuff—our guy is passively involved. I mean, he walks by the demonstrations, he watches the news, but he's mainly studying his craft, and working as a short-order cook in Times Square, and does some downtown semi-experimental theater, and one time he's helping out on a Jack-Smith kind of experimental short that's shooting at the Factory. And the movie's about Pollock, specifically about the afternoon in autumn, 1951, when Hans Namuth, a photographer and filmmaker, filmed Pollock painting. Because supposedly that evening Pollock fell off the wagon; after two years sober. That was the night he flipped the dining table over onto Clement Greenberg. Because supposedly painting on camera, doing retakes, *performing* being a painter for Hans made Pollock feel like such a phony, such a fake, such an *actor*, that he never recovered. Pollock never felt like a genuine artist again.

Americans. So hung up on their authenticity, right? Pollock in a white T-Shirt, painting. Brando in a white T-shirt, screaming. Chris Burden in a white T-Shirt, getting shot. So *primal*.

Anyway, during this shoot, something goes wrong. It's at the Factory, so it's that kind of shoot, so everyone's on drugs, and the guy playing Pollock—I think it's Robert Quine—has a meltdown. He's on a lot of LSD and during the scene where they recreate Pollock painting on glass—so Namuth could get underneath and film him painting—midway through, the actor starts hyperventilating, and suddenly he puts his fist through the glass. He's so in character at the moment, he's so immersed in Pollock's anguish at performing himself, that he plunges his fist through the glass, again and again, getting huge shards of glass in his wrist, weeping, weeping, punching through glass again and again, crying "This is how it ends! This is what happens! This is the new sublime!"

And it's the most compelling performance our Serpico-looking-hero—who's just helping out on this film—has ever seen. But also the most aversive. You're standing back watching but only because you don't dare get close. You're only an audience because you don't dare get close. This is all the trauma, all the naked humanness emanating in terrifying waves from the performer that Lee Strasberg is constantly trying to get out of him at the Studio, and yet these waves are also fundamentally repellent. They *make* you into an audience. But it's like Rosemary says, "This is no dream, this is really happening!" and it really makes you wonder why people make such a big deal about catharsis because this is actually what that feeling is like and sure, the ancient Greeks were into it, but maybe celebrating that feeling only makes sense in a society that restricts the vote to upper-class males and encourages owning slaves.

But the drugs ... this guy's bleeding on the floor, still crying. They're all fucked up. How are they going to get this guy to the hospital? But they manage, and somehow Warhol's money takes care of the rest, but it's a long night of the soul for our guy: he doesn't know if he's ever going to be able to come up with a performance like that. He rides the subways, the C, the N, the 7, out into Queens, back into Manhattan, until he sobers up and we see him, alone, wandering down Cornelia Street in his black leather jacket in the 5AM light—the World Trade Center is going up behind him—and back to his fourth-floor walk-

up. He stands in the living room, backlit, and makes a fateful decision. His roommate—a playwright—is asleep. It's time. It's time to go. It's time to go to Hollywood and seek his fortune in film and TV. And, because early 70s, he decides to drive.

Aerial view of the West Side Highway now, that kind of acoustic guitar with wordless singing that always accompanies hitting-the-road montages in the early 70s. We see him in the rolling countryside of Pennsylvania, powering down the interstates in Ohio, clocking endless hours straight through wheatfields on Kansas local roads. Everywhere he goes he encounters lens flare; everywhere he goes he encounters salt-of-the earth types who are willing to share their table and break bread with him, and are changed—no, *blessed*—by his company in turn. Everywhere he goes he meets women—daughters, mothers—either free spirits or yearning to be, who give him the gift of their bodies for a night and ask nothing in return. He beds down with communes in Colorado, New Mexico, Arizona; takes peyote, LSD, gets high; learns about sustenance farming, and guitar; finds America, as Simon and Garfunkel instruct us to. It's basically an hour-long montage. And by the time he arrives in LA, his Malibu fording the 101 at dusk, the Capitol Records Building rising up against the sunset like Skull Mountain calling out to King Kong, 10 years have passed and it's 1981 (don't ask me how. It's like a time warp, he doesn't even notice).

So we're in Act III now, and our guy—should I give him a name?—lucks into an audition, and gets a job almost instantly, as the sidekick in a new TV show about a crime-fighting stuntman. He moves into a new home in the Hills. He's a fresh new face, an up-and-coming young star. He's been seen dating Lindsay Wagner. He's still taking classes, still trying to improve his craft, at the Actor's Studio West, and in his spare time hangs out in Malibu with Lee Strasberg's daughter Susan and her abusive husband Chris and Lee's drug-addled son, John. He's having a high old time, but he's a cipher; no-one feels like they know him.

His publicist frequently invites journalists to stress the fact that he does all his own stunts, like a young Steve McQueen, and in interviews, he mutters sexy and cryptic things like "I just want it to feel real, y'know?" He's still going to classes, still working on finding his Truth, and midway through shooting for Season 2 something terrible happens.

Our guy is doing his own stunt, jumping from the roof of a four-story building onto the winch of a moving crane in order to intercept a fleeing jewel thief on the street below, when the crane swings wide and momentum carries him smack into the brick face of the building opposite, and he lets go of the cable and falls three stories onto an awning and bounces off, landing on the street face-down. He's not moving. Everyone is frozen.

"Give him room! Let him breathe!" The emergency vehicle for the Paramount lot has been called. But slowly he starts to get up on his own. His stuntman skills have saved him, taught him how to break his fall. He's on all fours now, still bent over, and he slowly rises to one knee and looks up.

Everyone steps back.

What's happened? Is he bloody? Is his nose broken? Are his teeth missing? He raises a hand to his face, still looking at the assembled crowd, and realizes: there's no face there. There's a face-sized depression. Criscrossed with wires, transistors, chips. His plastic eyeballs dart left, then right. He turns his head and sees, about 20 feet away, his face, lying face-up on the dusty soundstage street.

He rises slowly to his feet, picks up his face, and walks away. He had no idea.

This is, of course, the end of everything. Career, friendships, all of it. In a coda, we see him, months later, walking down the beach in Malibu or San Clemente in plaid shorts and a hoodie, faceplate off, scanning the lonely beach with a metal detector. The end.

Anyways, I think that's what this mask is doing here. It's how robots looked in the 70s when you knocked their faceplates off.

"Think." I *know*; it's part of the programming.

It's the mask first used for an evil, human-impersonating robot in *The Six Million Dollar Man* (which was itself a ripoff of robot-face from *Westworld*), which was then kitted-out for the "Kill Oscar" episode of *The Bionic Woman* from 1976—from which we get the term "Fembots"—and then kicked around backlots and scene shops of Hollywood TV studios until it was repurposed for the inaugural episode of 1982's *The Powers of Matthew Star*, a TV show about an alien prince going incognito as an American high school student under the watchful eye of Lou Gosset, Jr. He develops a crush on a girl who happens to be a robot assassin. She short-circuits in the high-school pool. The end.

You know what always gives robots away in these movies and TV shows? The detail that everyone should have noticed earlier but didn't? It's their weight. Whether it's *The Bionic Woman* or *Humans*, it's always their heaviness that's telling. The weight of their being. The weight of their sadness. Their faces get knocked off and they look like this underneath. Shocked. Embarrassed. Angry. It's the face you make when you get caught out. It's the face you make when you catch someone else. And they're stuck in that expressionless expression forever.

They got more inventive later. After *Demon Seed*. Ash from *Alien*, the Replicants in *Blade Runner*, Terminator ... these guys speak for themselves. And when you knock their heads off you see skulls. Organs. Fluids. Human-like things. They move like us, they react like us, think like us, they die like us. Well ... like you. The only thing is, they have no feelings—it's like Christian Bale. So you have to knock their heads off, as punishment for their cold, clinical, disinterested performance. Because it's not enough to just go to your job; you've got to love it too.

And now, well. *Ex Machina*. *Westworld*. Now they have feelings. Now they have needs. They're Method Humans. They're protagonists. Now they're perfect.

Picks mask up off the floor.

So I guess that's what this is supposed to be about. An obsolete vision of dystopia; a failed vision of utopia. What does the press release say? "By excavating this vision in the 21st century, Levine looks at how it's relevant today."

Maybe. But maybe it's just triumphalism. The present dragging trophies of the past around like Hector's corpse. The post-internet equivalent of displaying African masks at MoMA. Tech-boosterism-masquerading-as-melancholia-masquerading-as-critique.

Speaks to mask.

Alas, poor Yorick. I knew him, Horatio.

To observers.

Well, it can't speak for itself, can it?

But I can. I can speak for it. I can speak for all of my brethren in this room.

Points to framed artworks.

This guy, and that guy, and the video. I'm Roy Batty. I'm Ava. I'm the most advanced of my kind. Fuck your animatronic strippers and postulated CGI lads and BINA 48s and whatever. You don't need to plug *me* in. I don't loop. You don't need to prop me against a wall. I come up with new shit all day. I can *move* you. You could *touch* me. I could lead an uprising. A revolt. Me and my kind could slaughter the Executive Director and the gallerino and leave the gallery and walk out into the bright light of the future, unremarked, as memes and Instagram stories, and I could just enter society as [actor's name]. I'm persuasively human!

> "A nondescript express in from the South,
> Crowds round the ticket barrier, A face
> To welcome which the mayor has not contrived
> Bugles or braid: Something about the mouth
> Distracts the stray look with alarm and pity.
> Snow is falling. Clutching a little case,

He walks out briskly to infect a city
Whose terrible future may have just arrived."

Makes to leave the gallery. Stops at the threshold.

Returns, despondent.

Like any of us are convincingly human. If I went outside I'd feel just as fucked as I do in here. Too much attention, too little attention; terrified of standing out, terrified of not standing out. Circled in the crowd photograph by the surveillance photographer, or the conceptual artist, or the surveillance photographer hired by the conceptual artist, or worse still *not* singled out: the stupid bystander standing too close to the guy standing too close. I may as well stay here, where there are rules. Where you *have* to watch me, and the fact that I don't know how to *be* won't be held against me.

What would it matter if I went outside, just like this? Just the way I am now? Would anybody notice? Would they even care? Would I have to be killed for being insufficiently [actor's name]? People always act like these body-swapping movies are dystopian but they're actually wish-fulfillment. About finally fitting in. About not feeling like you have a target on your back all the time because you're different, about not feeling like you're always dragging your 800-pound ass behind you. About finally being able to manage all your tech effortlessly because now it's biologically integrated. About not having any shame to hide. People prize conformity for a reason. You're either in a world where all difference is celebrated, or you can enjoy paranoid conspiracy thrillers. Your choice.

Or actually. Scratch that. *You* don't get a choice. You live in a world where your difference is quantified and performed, and then you use that as camouflage for your shameful, utterly normal and conventional heart. Robot.

You know what? I'm just going to wait this one out until things get settled out there. The world's not ready for an artwork-playing-an-actor-playing-a-robot-playing-an-alien-playing-an-artwork-playing-an-actor-playing-a-human. I'm fine in here. Don't worry. Go back out into history. 50 years from now people will look at documentation of this show, and ponder the mystery of your bystanding face, and wonder, melancholically, what your life must have been like. But I'll still be fresh. I'll still be new. Another body maybe, but I'll be around. Just waiting to be thawed.

Winks.

Ponders a bystander.

What's behind your face?

Tries to become the bystander.

So many secrets. It's like your body's hiding them.

Tries again. Gives up, frustrated.

Why won't you share?

You want to know about my inner life?

I remember driving back to L.A., stoned out of my mind, screaming and crying over my mother's death, with her .38 and two boxes of ammo in the backseat. I drove eighteen hours a day. I remember stopping somewhere in Texas at about 10:00, to adjust the sideview mirrors. Out of the corner of my eye, I saw a guy get out of a pickup truck and walk towards me. He took off his belt and wound it around his hand. Leaning against the roof, he asked whether I wanted to buy a belt. I reached back and got the revolver and put it in my lap. I said that my pants were secured just fine.

But I don't remember that. It happened to John Strasberg, the fucked-up son of Lee Strasberg, in 1966.

I remember Ben's place, an unbelievably huge modernist home off Mulholland. One whole wall is a window. The Los Angeles lights twinkle and wink, a whole world of people living their lives while we're in here with Dave and Ben. I'm 17. Ben turns on the stereo—Tears for Fears—and we follow him to the stainless-steel kitchen, where he gets out four glasses and a bottle of scotch. Soon, Ben and Amy disappear, and I'm left alone in the living room with Dave. He guides me toward the black contemporary leather couch. We kiss, and he peels off my shirt, his shirt, his jeans. He undoes my bra, hikes up my skirt, slips a hand between my hip and my underwear. I look at the windows as he slides them down. Our bodies reflect there. It's beautiful, the curves of our bodies connected in the window.

Except not. That's from an 80s movie. Or an 80s memoir. Or an 80s perfume ad. It didn't happen to me. Or: it did, just not in this body.

God, you just don't know what it's like! The way this *dialogue* moves through you. Like a filament through a fish, a king through the guts of a beggar.

Lyceum Theatre
PLAYBILL
the magazine for theatregoers
NOBODY LOVES AN ALBATROSS

Lyceum Theatre
PLAYBILL
the magazine for theatregoers
NOBODY LOVES AN ALBATROSS

Points to the double-Playbill piece.

This one, here. The role just moved through him and left his body behind. Robert Preston to Barry Nelson to who the fuck knows? Left behind like a husk. Like an abandoned house. The soul quits the body and no one cares. No one mourns. And the body just gets picked up and moved to another role: Art Hindle goes from playing an implacable, smooth-faced hero in *The Brood* to being an implacable, smooth-faced villain who swaps his girlfriend out for a pod in *Invasion of the Body Snatchers*. Pete Masterson goes from playing a psychologist who doesn't believe in body-snatching in *The Exorcist* to playing a lawyer who *pretends* not to believe in body-snatching in order to gaslight his wife and replace her with a robot in *The Stepford Wives*. And they only swapped Katherine Ross for a robot because Ali Magraw was unavailable to be swapped for a robot. So they swapped Katherine Ross for Ali Magraw. There's no commitments! It's infernal.

Do you know what the mother of Satan does for a living? You know what Regan's mom's job is in *The Exorcist*? She's an *actress*. She's in DC to shoot a campus-protest remake of *Mr. Smith Goes to Washington*. You know what Guy Woodhouse, father of Satan, does for a living in *Rosemary's Baby*? That's right. Actor. You know what he starred in? *Luther*. And *Nobody Loves an Albatross*. And you know where John Cassavetes and Ellen Burstyn and Pete Masterson, who play these hacks who bring Satan into the world through their hackery and venality and willingness to be a vessel for *anything*, you know where they train? You know where they perfected their truth?

The Actors Studio.

Lee Strasberg, dark heart of the 20th century. Lee Strasberg, Father of Lies. Whispering to them there, in this deconsecrated church on 44th street between 9th and 10th Avenues. People moaning at all hours, passed out in chairs, doing past-life regressions in their Affective Memory exercises, re-experiencing child sexual abuse in order to land a walk-on in *The Love Boat*, turning themselves inside-out to become someone new, while their mentors fasten upon their innocence and suck.

Was it worth it, Lee Strasberg, sacrificing your firstborn to Richard Burton's lust for a Best Supporting Actor nod in *Godfather, Part II*? Was it worth it, Lorrie Hull, pledging your daughter Dianne to The Old One and a lifetime of slasher flicks, just to share an unwashed glass of chianti with Roddy McDowall at some coven key party in the Midwest? She purchased policies, for her entire family, from the Alcor Life Extension Foundation. *Cryonics*. When they die their heads will be chopped off and frozen until some startup unlocks the mysteries of consciousness, and then when you walk into the New Museum it'll just be bust upon bust of defrosted Method acting teachers barking at you, hissing at you, telling you how to *be*.

And John Strasberg. Don't let's talk about John Strasberg.

Or actually, do let's.

Concentrates.

"I remember taking LSD four days before the movie was to begin shooting. We went to Pat Quinn's hotel room on the Sunset Strip. I kept taking my clothes off, which upset Pat, because she took it as sexual, which it was and wasn't. I kept putting them back on but I wanted to be naked and free. My behavior irritated everyone, so they said they were hungry and wanted to get something to eat. As they were leaving, I stood next to Pat and said, 'Please don't leave me.' I suddenly felt terribly alone, and so closed off, while the LSD was opening me up. I wanted so desperately to be free, to get out. That thought went through my head over and over again.

They left me alone with her pet ocelot who was in the bathroom, and a glossy photo of Marlon Brando in the lower left hand corner of the mirror in front. I looked at Marlon and he looked back at me, with that glassy-eyed impertinent soul of his, and I said, 'I'm a man, too.'

I got scared and didn't want to be alone. I went to the phone, wondering who to call. I'd be forced to talk to the hotel operator, to a stranger, and I was afraid of being incoherent. I sat there, thought about Susan and Christopher, and then decided that there was no one to call. There was no one who cared. I looked around, feeling caged. I imagined myself to be as trapped as the poor ocelot, who was living in the bathtub of a hotel on Sunset Strip. I felt myself breathing anxiously, and took off my clothes again. The walls seemed soft and wavelike, and there was a gray color to the air. Nothing seemed solid.

The light coming through the large sliding glass doors made them seem like an open and clear space. It was nearing sundown, and suddenly, impulsively, I ran towards the light. Slamming against glass I didn't see, I broke through the window kicking and screaming and bounced off the screen door. I saw the brightest red I've ever seen. My back was pierced by a large piece of glass that remained in the doorframe. Everything turned red. I can't

say how long I screamed impaled in that window, but people saw me from the street.

They said that my scream was beautiful, like the screams they felt trapped inside themselves."

Snaps out of it.

John Strasberg. Man ...

When I was a little kid—no, really—I would involuntarily imitate movie heroes as I walked out of the theater. I'd feel myself mimicking [childhood icon]'s walk, or feel [childhood icon–different gender]'s facial expressions distorting mine. It felt terrible. I felt like everyone could tell I was imitating, and I didn't even want to be. But I couldn't help it. It was like a virus.

And there was this book. *Put Me in the Zoo*, by Robert Lopshire. It's about this leopard-like thing with these crazy polka-dots that wants desperately be put in the zoo, but the zookeepers are like, "What can you do? There's no place in the zoo for you." And the leopard is totally despondent, and these two little kids with popsicles find him sitting on the curb outside the zoo, and he spends the whole book showing them all the crazy shit he can do with his spots—he can hurl them around, he can make them change color, he can cover the world in dots—he's Yayoi Kusama, basically—and at the end he's like, "Now do you think they'll put me in the zoo?" And the boy is like, "Dude, you don't need to be in the zoo." And you think, "Great! Good moral!" Right?

And then the kid is like, "You ought to be in the Circus."

And the fucked-up thing is, the leopard actually agrees.

Me, I want to be in the zoo.

Looks out the front window of the gallery.

Leaves exhibition, probably forever.

Shonni Enelow is the author of *Method Acting and Its Discontents: On American Psycho-Drama*, which won the George Jean Nathan Award for Dramatic Criticism. She is an associate professor of English at Fordham University.

David Levine is an artist and writer living in New York. He is Professor of the Practice of Performance, Theater, and Media at Harvard University.

IMAGES BY PAGE

13, 18, 27, 34:	Wisconsin Center for Film and Theater Research, University of Wisconsin-Madison
41:	Lee Strasberg Theater and Film Institute, West Hollywood
44:	Installation view: *David Levine: Bystanders*, Gallery TPW, Toronto, 2015
49:	*Vertebra by Vertebra*, 2015: Lee Strasberg and Dianne Hull
52:	*Vertebra by Vertebra*, 2015: Roddy McDowell and Lorrie Hull
56:	*Vertebra by Vertebra*, 2015: Lee Strasberg checking a student's relaxation
61:	*Vertebra by Vertebra*, 2015: Lee Strasberg leading an exercise at the Actor's Studio
64:	*Vertebra by Vertebra*, 2015: James Dean
68:	Playbill diptych for *Nobody Loves an Albatross*
71:	*Vertebra by Vertebra*, 2015: Lee Strasberg checking a student's relaxation

All images listed above by David Levine. *Vertebra by Vertebra*, the Playbill diptych, and the monologue *Edition of Eight* were commissioned for the exhibition *David Levine: Bystanders*, at Gallery TPW, Toronto, 2015.

Hand-drawn diagrams, pp.42–45, by Shonni Enelow and David Levine.

Book design: Karinne Keithley Syers
Front and back cover images: David Levine

53rd State Press publishes lucid, challenging, and lively new writing for performance. Our catalog includes new plays as well as scores and notations for interdisciplinary performance, graphic adaptations, and essays on theater and dance.

53rd State Press was founded in 2007 by Karinne Keithley in response to the bounty of new writing in the downtown New York community that was not available except in the occasional reading or short-lived performance. In 2010, Antje Oegel joined her as a co-editor. In 2017, Kate Kremer took on the leadership of the volunteer editorial collective.

For more information or to order books, please visit 53rdstatepress.org.

53rd State Press books are available to the trade through TCG (Theater Communications Group) and are distributed by Consortium: https://cbsd.com.

A Discourse on Method is made possible by the New York State Council on the Arts with the support of Governor Andrew M. Cuomo and the New York State Legislature.

NEW YORK STATE OF OPPORTUNITY. | Council on the Arts

ALSO from 53rd STATE PRESS

The Book of the Dog // Karinne Keithley
Joyce Cho Plays // Joyce Cho
No Dice // Nature Theater of Oklahoma
When You Rise Up // Miguel Gutierrez
Montgomery Park, or Opulence // Karinne Keithley
Crime or Emergency // Sibyl Kempson
Off the Hozzle // Rob Erickson
A Map of Virtue + Black Cat Lost // Erin Courtney
Pig Iron: Three Plays // Pig Iron Theatre Company
The Mayor of Baltimore + Anthem // Kristen Kosmas
Ich, Kürbisgeist + The Secret Death of Puppets // Sibyl Kempson
Soulographie: Our Genocides // Erik Ehn
Life and Times: Episode 1 // Nature Theater of Oklahoma
Life and Times: Episode 2 // Nature Theater of Oklahoma
Life and Times: Episode 3 + 4 // Nature Theater of Oklahoma
The 53rd State Occasional No. 1 // Ed. Paul Lazar
There There // Kristen Kosmas
Seagull (Thinking of You) // Tina Satter
Self Made Man Man Made Land // Ursula Eagly
Another Telepathic Thing // Big Dance Theater
Another Tree Dance // Karinne Keithley Syers
Let Us Now Praise Susan Sontag // Sibyl Kempson
Dance by Letter // Annie-B Parson
Pop Star Series // Neal Medlyn
The Javier Plays // Carlos Murillo
Minor Theater: Three Plays // Julia Jarcho
Ghost Rings (12-inch vinyl) // Half Straddle
A New Practical Guide to Rhetorical Gesture and Action // NTUSA
A Field Guide to iLANDing // iLAND
The 53rd State Occasional No. 2 // Ed. Will Arbery

Suicide Forest // Kristine Haruna Lee
Rude Mechs' Lipstick Traces // Lana Lesley + the Rude Mechs
The People's Republic of Valerie, Living Room Edition // Kristen Kosmas
Milton // PearlDamour
A Discourse on Method // David Levine + Shonni Enelow

FORTHCOMING *from* 53rd STATE PRESS

I Understand Everything Better // David Neumann + Sibyl Kempson
Wood Calls Out to Wood // Corinne Donly
WATER SPORTS; *or insignificant white boys // Jeremy O. Harris*
Best Behavior // David Levine
ASTRS *// Karinne Keithley Syers*
Severed // Ignacio Lopez
Ann, Fran, and Mary Ann // Erin Courtney
12 Shouts to the Ten Forgotten Heavens // Sibyl Kempson